THE LITTLE GUIDE TO
MONTY PYTHON

Published in 2024 by OH!
An Imprint of Welbeck Non-Fiction Limited,
part of Welbeck Publishing Group.
Offices in: London – 20 Mortimer Street, London W1T 3JW
and Sydney – Level 17, 207 Kent St, Sydney NSW 2000 Australia
www.welbeckpublishing.com

Compilation text © Welbeck Non-Fiction Limited 2024
Design © Welbeck Non-Fiction Limited 2024

Disclaimer:
All trademarks, company names, brand names, registered names, quotations, scripted text, characters, logos, dialogues and catchphrases used or cited in this book are the property of their respective owners and are mentioned in this book within quotation fair dealings or used as cultural references or for identity, review and guidance purpose only. The publisher does not assume and hereby disclaim any liability to any party for any loss, damage or disruption caused by errors or omissions, whether such errors or omissions result from negligence, accident or any other cause. This book is a publication of *OH! An imprint of Welbeck Publishing Group Limited* and has not been licensed, approved, sponsored, or endorsed by any person or entity.

All rights reserved. No part of this publication may be reproduced, stored in a retrieval system, or transmitted in any form or by any means (including electronic, mechanical, photocopying, recording, or otherwise) without prior written permission from the publisher.

ISBN 978-1-80069-583-2

Compiled and written by: Malcolm Croft
Editorial: Victoria Denne
Designer: Tony Seddon
Project manager: Russell Porter
Production: Arlene Lestrade

A CIP catalogue record for this book is available from the British Library

Printed in Dubai

10 9 8 7 6 5 4 3 2 1

IT'S...

THE LITTLE GUIDE TO

MONTY PYTHON

COMPLETELY UNOFFICIAL
AND UNAUTHORIZED

OH!

CONTENTS

INTRODUCTION – 6

8

CHAPTER
ONE

NIPPLES EXPLODING
WITH DELIGHT

78

CHAPTER
TWO

SHRUBBERIES &
ELDERBERRIES

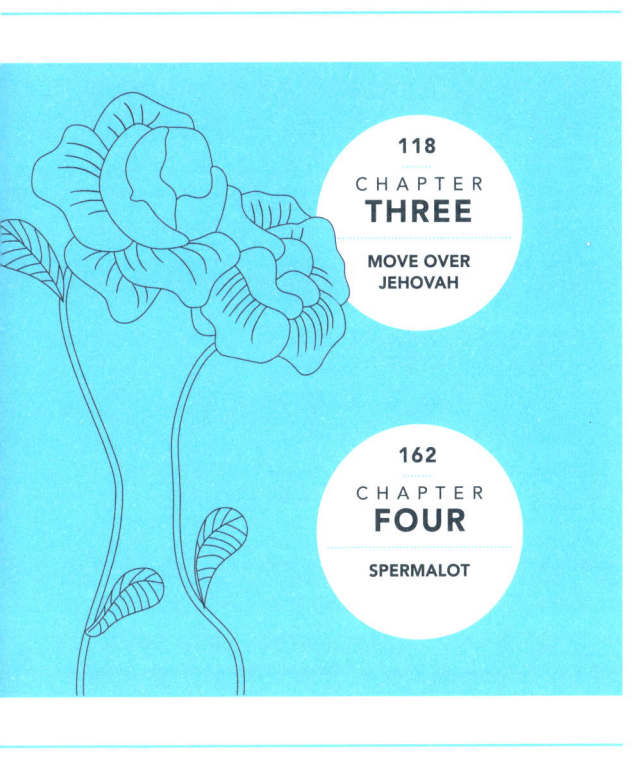

118

CHAPTER
THREE

MOVE OVER JEHOVAH

162

CHAPTER
FOUR

SPERMALOT

INTRODUCTION

Since their arrival in the late 1960s, Monty Python have been to blame for a comedy revolution that not only defied the limits of British sensibilities, it *defiled* them, leaving a wet spot so immense that future generations are defined and drenched forever in their influence. Yes, these "Beatles of Comedy" are as immortal as they are inspirational, as innovative as they are intelligent, and as incomparable as they are, er, um, insert a word beginning with 'in' here. For more than 50 years, their original brand of ensemble silliness has circumnavigated the world more times than Michael Palin's toothbrush, their legacy remaining erect for each new generation to gaze upon in awe.

The group's genius lies in its fusion of zany lunacy and profound existentialism, a hyper-intellectual immaturity hitherto never seen before on UK TV; they struck a major chord with the fast-changing 1970s counterculture immediately, rightly ridiculing the foundational institutions of snobby British society just as the potential for colour TV kicked in. As Michael Palin said, "Monty Python was a child's way of deconstructing television."

On the eve of 40 years since their last true masterpiece, 1983's *The Meaning of Life*, was born, this compact compendium is here to celebrate every morsel of the troupe's output. This tiny tome may be perhaps the only time you ever expect the Spanish inquisition to arrive (see P33), so, you're welcome. It's certainly the only time you'll see silly walks, ex-parrots (and ex-lepers), fish-slapping, spam, shrubberies, and, of course, ocelot spleens, under the same umbrella, all curated expertly from Monty Python's mighty canon – *Flying Circus*, *Holy Grail*, *Life of Brian*, and *Meaning of Life* – as well as a few other bits and sods we found lying around.

Made from the paper of the mightiest tree and cut to size with a herring, this *Little Guide* may be only ever-so-slightly bigger than a wafer-thin mint, but it's packed with enough preposterous comedy power to keep proper Pythonites stuffed with silliness until Mr Big Nose is taken away for crucifixion. So, if you're ready, let's begin.

NIPPLES EXPLODING WITH DELIGHT

❧

The circus is in town! It's time for a joyride inside the silly-filled mind of Monty Python, the brainchild of six loonies who stole the keys to the asylum.

Let's kickstart this cute collection of quotes with something completely normal (nobody's expecting that!) – the greatest gags pulled from the 45 episodes of genius that complete Monty Python's Flying Circus. Hold onto your spam, it's going to get very, very flipperwaldt gersput!

NIPPLES EXPLODING WITH DELIGHT

And what exactly are the commercial possibilities of ovine aviation?

The Tourist and the Shepherd discuss flying sheep,
Monty Python's Flying Circus, 1969–1974.

When we couldn't figure out what to write about, we would take a thesaurus and I would read words out. Graham would say, 'I like plummet.' I said, 'So do I. It's a funny word.' Pffffft . . . splat! 'So what would plummet?' He said, 'A sheep would plummet, if it tried to fly.' Then we had the flying sheep sketch.

John Cleese, on the lunacy of language helping write sketches, *New Yorker*, interview with Michael Shulman, September 20, 2020.

NIPPLES EXPLODING WITH DELIGHT

Eh? Know what I mean? Know what I mean? Nudge, nudge! Know what I mean? Say no more! A nod's as good as a wink to a blind bat, say no more, say no more!

Arthur Nudge, on sex (presumably), *Monty Python's Flying Circus*, 1969–1974.

The other Pythons all lead boring lives, but Graham lives what we do on the screen for real.

Terry Gilliam, on Graham Chapman,
Late Night with David Letterman, June 24, 1982.

NIPPLES EXPLODING WITH DELIGHT

Welcome aboard, Britisher pig. Quite a little surprise, ja? But perhaps you would be so kind as to tell us how you know about certain allied shipping routes, ja? Come on, talk!

The Nazi Fish, to the freshly gulped Michael Palin, following his fish dance slap, *Monty Python's Flying Circus*, 1969–1974.

HALIBUT (LARGE)

The species of fish used by John Cleese's soldier to thwack Michael Palin's soldier into Teddington Lock in the "Fish Slapping Dance" sketch. Palin started the fight with two tiny pilchards.

OCTOBER 5, 1969 10.55PM

The night comedy, and television, changed forever. It was the debut broadcast of episode one of *Monty Python's Flying Circus*, a month before the BBC announced a full service of colour television.

> Nine out of 10 British housewives can't tell the difference between Whizzo Butter and a dead crab.

Palin's Interviewer meets the Pepperpots (who threaten to slit his face!), *Monty Python's Flying Circus*, 1969–1974.

NIPPLES EXPLODING WITH DELIGHT

The BBC didn't quite know what to do with us and so they rather nervously gave us a free hand to create our own program.

Graham Chapman, on *Flying Circus*, interview with the *New York Times*, 1976.

> I must warn you, sir, that outside I have police dog Josephine, who is not only armed and trained to sniff out certain substances but is also a junkie.

Police Constable Henry Thatcher interrogates Sandy Camp before E. B. Debenham (Mrs) complains to the BBC about the silly sketch, *Monty Python's Flying Circus*, 1969–1974.

NIPPLES EXPLODING WITH DELIGHT

Why is it the world never remembered the name of Johann Gambolputty de von Ausfern-schplenden-schlitter-crasscrenbon-fried-digger-dangle-dongle-dungle-burstein-von-knacker-thrasher-apple-banger-horowitz-ticolensicgrander-knotty-spelltinkle-grandlich-grumblemeyer-spelterwasser-kurstlich-himbleeisen-bahnwagen-gutenabend-bitte-ein-nürnburger-bratwurstle-gerspurten-mit-zwei-macheluber-hundsfut-gumberaber-shoenendanker-kalbsfleisch-mittler-aucher von Hautkopft of Ulm?

Mr Figgis pines for a particular decomposing composer, *Monty Python's Flying Circus*, 1969–1974.

NIPPLES EXPLODING WITH DELIGHT

Five episodes are definitely cringe-worthy and I suppose another five or so are a little below par, and about a third of the rest are pretty good. And the rest: really, really, quite good.

Graham Chapman, on the 45 episodes of *Flying Circus*, from *A Critical Look at Python*, 2006.

For the very first show, the audience consisted of a lot of old-age pensioners who actually thought they were coming to see a real circus. They were a bit puzzled.

Terry Jones, on *Flying Circus*, interview with Mike Sacks, *Vulture*, January 2014.

NIPPLES EXPLODING WITH DELIGHT

Now, I've noticed a tendency for this program to get rather silly. Now I do my best to keep things moving along, but I'm not having things getting silly. Those last two sketches I did get very silly indeed!

The Colonel warns the film crew, before stopping the Two Hermits sketch (for getting too silly), *Monty Python's Flying Circus*, 1969–1974.

I didn't want to be a barber anyway. I wanted to be a lumberjack! Leaping from tree to tree as they float down the mighty rivers of British Columbia! The giant Red-Wood, the Larch, the Fur, the mighty Scott's Pine! The smell of fresh cut timber! The crash of mighty trees! With my best girlie by my side! And we'd sing, sing…SING!

Bevis the Barber (AKA, the Lumberjack) prepares to break into song, *Monty Python's Flying Circus*, 1969–1974.

NIPPLES EXPLODING WITH DELIGHT

'E's not pinin'! 'E's passed on! This parrot is no more! He has ceased to be! 'E's expired and gone to meet 'is maker! 'E's a stiff! Bereft of life, 'e rests in peace! If you hadn't nailed 'im to the perch 'e'd be pushing up the daisies! 'Is metabolic processes are now 'istory! 'E's off the twig! 'E's kicked the bucket, 'e's shuffled off 'is mortal coil, run down the curtain and joined the bleedin' choir invisible!

THIS IS AN EX-PARROT!

Mr Praline complains to the pet shop owner about the lifeless symptoms of his Norwegian Blue, *Monty Python's Flying Circus*, 1969–1974.

NIPPLES EXPLODING WITH DELIGHT

If I said you had a beautiful body, would you hold it against me… I am no longer infected.

Hungarian Man tries his best to speak English with a Tobacconist using a Dirty Hungarian Phrasebook, *Monty Python's Flying Circus*, 1969–1974.

It's Deirdre.

Mr Pewtey, to the Marriage Counsellor, about his ravishing wife's name, "soft and gentle, warm and yielding, deeply lyrical and yet tender (and frightened like a tiny white rabbit)", *Monty Python's Flying Circus*, 1969–1974.

NIPPLES EXPLODING WITH DELIGHT

What's brown and sounds like a bell?

Dung!

©Arthur Name, *Monty Python's Flying Circus*, 1969–1974.

Good riddance to him, the freeloading bastard, I hope he fries! And the reason I feel I should say this, is he would never forgive me if I didn't, if I threw away this glorious opportunity to shock you all on his behalf. Anything for him, but mindless good taste.

John Cleese, at Graham Chapman's memorial service, 1989.

NIPPLES EXPLODING WITH DELIGHT

Mr Wentworth just told me to come in here and say that there was trouble at the mill, that's all! I didn't expect a kind of Spanish Inquisition!

Reg never expected the Spanish Inquisition
(as the Spanish Inquisition burst through the door),
Monty Python's Flying Circus, 1969–1974.

Nobody expects the Spanish Inquisition!

Cardinal Ximénez (with Fang and Biggles by his side) to poor unexpecting Reg, *Monty Python's Flying Circus*, 1969–1974.

* *"Their chief weapon is surprise! Surprise and fear. Fear and surprise. Their two weapons are fear and surprise – and ruthless efficiency! Their three weapons are fear, and surprise, and ruthless efficiency, and an almost fanatical devotion to the Pope. Their four weapons are such elements as fear, surpr–"*

NIPPLES EXPLODING WITH DELIGHT

Mike Palin wrote 'The Spanish Inquisition'. How did Mike go from England in 1911 to then having three torturers from the fifteenth century burst into the sitting room and announce, 'Nobody expects the Spanish Inquisition'? Where did he make that connection? And how did he make it work? In the end, you get a laugh. But when you reverse-engineer it, it's quite hard to follow how he came up with the original spark, the original idea. And yet it still works.

Terry Jones, on "The Spanish Inquisition", interview with Mike Sacks, *Vulture*, January 2014.

MAY 11, 1969

The day Monty Python was born at the Light of Kashmir tandoori restaurant, Hampstead, London. Graham, John, Eric, Terry J, Michael and Terry G met to discuss working on a new BBC comedy series together.

NIPPLES EXPLODING WITH DELIGHT

DECEMBER 8, 2010

The day Elon Musk rocketed a giant wheel of Le Brouére cheese into orbit as a maiden test payload for SpaceX's Dragon space capsule, aboard a Falcon Rocket. He later revealed it was "the silliest thing he could think, and inspired by Monty Python", presumably the "Cheese Shop Sketch" from Flying Circus.

> I'm sorry to have kept you waiting but my walk has become rather sillier lately so it takes me a rather long time to arrive.

Mr Teabag to Mr Pewtey, at the Ministry of Silly Walks, *Monty Python's Flying Circus*, 1969–1974.

11 MINUTES

John Cleese's Silly Walk is a great way to get fit. According to Forbes, 11 minutes a day of silly walking is enough to fulfil the 75 minutes of vigorous physical activity per week required for adults to maintain good health.

> You know, there are many people in the country today who, through no fault of their own, are sane. Some of them were born sane. Some of them became sane later in their lives. It is up to people like you and me, who are out of our tiny little minds, to help these people overcome their sanity.

Reverend Arthur Belling of St Looney Up-The-Cream-Bun-and-Jam goes full bananas, following a BBC voiceover for sanity, *Monty Python's Flying Circus*, 1969–1974.

NIPPLES EXPLODING WITH DELIGHT

> It's just gone eight o'clock and time for the penguin on top of your television set to explode.

A TV Announcer's inspired guess about the butch-looking "Penguin on the Television", *Monty Python's Flying Circus*, 1969–1974.

> **Dressing up as decrepit old ladies, and even decrepit young ladies, was one of our staples.**

Graham Chapman, on the troupe's love of female clothing, *A Liar's Autobiography*, 1980.

NIPPLES EXPLODING WITH DELIGHT

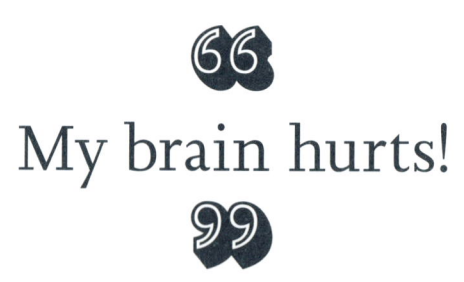

> **My brain hurts!**

D. P. Gumby informs Doctor Gumby of his symptoms, *Monty Python's Flying Circus*, 1969–1974.

> Well, I've been in the city for 30 years and I've never once regretted being a nasty, greedy, cold-hearted, avaricious money-grubber… er, Conservative!

Fourth City Gent gets political in the "City Gents" sketch, *Monty Python's Flying Circus*, 1969–1974.

NIPPLES EXPLODING WITH DELIGHT

> Spam, Spam, Spam, Spam… Lovely Spam! Wonderful Spam!

The Vikings interrupt Mr and Mrs Bun's order of spam, egg, sausage and spam (that's not got much spam in it) at the Green Midget cafe, *Monty Python's Flying Circus*, 1969–1974.

> There was one occasion when John Cleese and myself actually felt guilty about laughing at something we were writing, because it was in incredibly bad taste. So bad was the taste that we just couldn't help laughing at it. It concerned a gentleman walking into an undertaker's premises with his dead mother in a sack. And from there it got worse.

Graham Chapman, on the notorious "Dead Mother" sketch, *Late Night with David Letterman*, June 24, 1982.

NIPPLES EXPLODING WITH DELIGHT

> Look, we'll eat her, and if you're feeling a bit guilty about it afterwards, we'll dig a grave and you can throw up in it!

The Undertaker pushes the boundaries of bad taste in Python's most notorious sketch, *Monty Python's Flying Circus*, 1969–1974.

> Argument is an intellectual process. Contradiction is just the automatic gainsaying of anything the other person says.*

Palin's Man is spoiling for a dispute in the iconic "Argument Clinic" sketch, *Monty Python's Flying Circus*, 1969–1974.

*"It is NOT!"

3.4 BILLION

The number of spam, or junk, emails sent every day worldwide, roughly 48 per cent of all daily emails. It is called spam thanks to the "Spam" sketch.

Spam is a brand name of luncheon meat made popular in the 1960s, a contraction of the words "spiced ham".

> My view of the world really is that if you screw your eyes up and look at the world, it is an absurd and extraordinarily silly place, with everyone taking themselves very seriously.

Michael Palin, on the state of the world, interview with Bryan Appleyard, *Sunday Times*, September 9, 2018.

NIPPLES EXPLODING WITH DELIGHT

> Now I'm arrestin' this entire show on three counts:
> **One:** acts of self-conscious behaviour contrary
> to the 'Not in front of the children' Act,
> **Two:** always saying 'It's so and so of the Yard'
> every time the fuzz arrives and,
> **Three:** and this is the cruncher, offences
> against the 'Getting out of sketches
> without using a proper punchline' Act,
> **Four:** namely, simply ending every bleedin'
> sketch by just having a policeman come in…
> and… wait a minute.

Inspector Fox of the Light Entertainment Police, Comedy Division, Special Flying Squad, arrests the Spreaders under Section 21 of the Strange Sketch Act, before realising what's happening, *Monty Python's Flying Circus*, 1969–1974.

> Well, ladies and gentlemen, I don't think any of our contestants tonight succeeded in encapsulating the intricacies of Proust's masterwork. So, I'm going to give the award to the girl with the biggest tits.

Arthur Mee declares the winner in the "Summarize Proust Competition", *Monty Python's Flying Circus*, 1969–1974.

NIPPLES EXPLODING WITH DELIGHT

In 2003, a fairly conclusive poll by Channel 4 revealed the Greatest Comedy Sketches of all time naturally included three Python sketches in the top 20 – "Dead Parrot", "Spanish Inquisition" and "Ministry of Silly Walks".

> The show was the star, and we all just were working for it. We were constantly fighting, but we were fighting over the right things – the quality of the material… whether it was good, whether it was funny, whether it worked.

Terry Gilliam, on creating *Flying Circus*, interview with Ken Plume, *IGN*, November 15, 2000.

NIPPLES EXPLODING WITH DELIGHT

> At the very beginning, Monty Python was largely inspired by the end of the British Empire. When I was a child, Britain had just gone through WWII, but it still ruled half the world. In the space of a few years, it all changed completely. The Army, the church, all the political institutions and their stuffy attitudes lost a lot of their power. Python was part of the disrespectful bunch which helped to mock the establishment.

Michael Palin, on the fall of the British Empire, interview with Bryan Appleyard, *Sunday Times*, September 6, 2014.

> I had incredible freedom – more than the others, in a sense, in the show – because what I did was completely different from what they did, so I didn't have to submit my ideas to the group. I used to turn up on the days we recorded with a can of film under my arm, and in it went.

Terry Gilliam, on animating for *Flying Circus*, interview with Ken Plume, *IGN*, November 15, 2000.

6.7

A recent gait analysis study revealed that John Cleese's silly walk is 6.7 times sillier than standard human walking.

> The BBC would like to apologize to everyone in the world for that last item. It was disgusting and bad and thoroughly disobedient, and please don't bother to phone up because we know it was very tasteless, but the Pythons didn't really mean it and they all come from broken homes and have very unhappy personal lives, especially Eric.

Announcer #1 apologizes on behalf of the BBC for Monty Python's tasteless sketches, *Monty Python's Flying Circus*, 1969–1974.

NIPPLES EXPLODING WITH DELIGHT

> I think that was our genius: we could do crap better than anybody else and get away with it.

Terry Gilliam, on *Flying Circus*, *Time Out*, June 16, 2014.

> **Make tea, not love.**

Hell's Grannies, *Monty Python's Flying Circus*, 1969–1974.

NIPPLES EXPLODING WITH DELIGHT

THE FUNNIEST JOKE IN THE WORLD

Wenn ist das Nunstück git und Slotermeyer?

Ja! Beiherhund das oder die Flipperwaldt gersput!

©Ernest Scribbler, writer of jokes (deceased),
Monty Python's Flying Circus, 1969–1974.

> Now, it's quite simple to deal with a banana fiend. First, you force him to drop the banana. Then, you eat the banana, thus disarming him. You have now rendered him helpless!

Self-Defence Against Fresh Fruit (not bunches) teacher, *Monty Python's Flying Circus*, 1969–1974.

NIPPLES EXPLODING WITH DELIGHT

> Mount Everest. Forbidding. Aloof. Terrifying. The mountain with the biggest tits in the world.

The Narrator narrates, before having to start again, as the International Hairdressers Expedition makes their ascent, *Monty Python's Flying Circus*, 1969–1974.

> **It's nice to see that look of alarm on the faces of the others.**

Graham Chapman, on creating controversial comedy, *A Liar's Autobiography*, 1980.

NIPPLES EXPLODING WITH DELIGHT

> In this picture, there are forty-seven people. None of them can be seen. In this film, we hope to show you how not to be seen. This is Mr E. R. Bradshaw of Napier Court, Black Lion Road, London, SE14. He cannot be seen. Now I'm going to ask him to stand up. Mr Bradshaw, will you stand up, please?

The Announcer demonstrates the value of not being seen (by shooting poor Mr Bradshaw dead), *Monty Python's Flying Circus*, 1969–1974.

Terry Gilliam's animated giant foot that squashes the title card of Monty Python's *Flying Circus* before the start of each show actually belongs to none other than the Roman god of love, Cupid. The foot is taken from the Renaissance painting "Venus, Cupid, Folly and Time" by Bronzino.

NIPPLES EXPLODING WITH DELIGHT

> Our first rule was: no punchlines. Some sketches start brilliant, great acting, really funny sketch, but the punchline is just not as good as the rest of the sketch, so it kills the entire thing. That's why we eliminated them.

Terry Gilliam, on the lack of Python punchlines, *Monty Python Live in Aspen*, 2007.

Before Monty Python decided on a name for their first BBC TV show, *Flying Circus*, they offered the BBC a list of silly titles as a joke, including "Owl Stretching Time", "The Toad Elevating Moment", "A Horse, a Spoon, and a Basin", "Bumwacket, Buzzard, Stubble and Boot". "Flying Circus" was only used because the BBC printed their programming schedules with the name already in it and it could no longer be changed.

NIPPLES EXPLODING WITH DELIGHT

> It was tremendously difficult to keep up that level of quality with Python. We made it a point to end sketches when they might have just been beginning on other shows. Writing was very serious business; we took it very seriously. But it did take a lot out of us.

Terry Jones, on writing for Python, interview with Mike Sacks, *Vulture*, January 2014.

> What makes it worse is that sometimes at the end of a sentence, I'll come out with the wrong fuse box...and ash trays your uncle. I won't be strawberry about it.

Mr Burrows struggles to discuss his speaking issues with Dr E. Henry Thripshaw, *Monty Python's Flying Circus*, 1969–1974.

NIPPLES EXPLODING WITH DELIGHT

> At the end of the *Do Not Adjust Your Set* (1968) series, Mike, Eric, Terry, and myself were all more and more a team wanting to do something together. Cleese had a standing invitation from the BBC to do a show if he ever wanted to, and he was keen to work with Mike Palin. So John and Graham – who wrote together – came together with us and we took up the offer with the BBC… and that was *Monty Python's Flying Circus*.

Terry Gilliam, on the genesis of Monty Python, interview with Ken Plume, *IGN*, November 15, 2000.

> Good evening. Tonight on *Is There?* we examine the question, 'Is there a life after death?' And here to discuss it are three dead people.

Roger Last interviews the very late Sir Brian Hardacre, Professor Thynne and Prebendary Reverend Ross on being dead, *Monty Python's Flying Circus*, 1969–1974.

NIPPLES EXPLODING WITH DELIGHT

> Oh we used to dream of livin' in a corridor! Woulda' been a palace to us. We used to live in an old water tank on a rubbish tip. We got woken up every morning by having a load of rotting fish dumped all over us.

The Four Yorkshiremen attempt to one-up-man each other, "The Four Yorkshiremen" sketch, *Monty Python Live at the Hollywood Bowl*, 1982.

"The Liberty Bell March", the troupe's iconic theme song, is by John Philip Sousa, an American lovingly known as the "March King". The tune was picked by Terry Gilliam because it had fallen into public domain and was free to use.

NIPPLES EXPLODING WITH DELIGHT

> The six of us produced a harmony that was somebody else. We'd write together, and we were almost writing for this seventh voice. There was always that image of another voice that was there. It was the Python voice, really. And it couldn't quite be duplicated with any other combination – or alone. With Python, we had a lot of different minds at work, and we worked very well together.

Terry Jones, on writing for Python, interview with Mike Sacks, *Vulture*, January 2014.

> Right! Stop that! It's SILLY. Very SILLY indeed! Started off as a nice little idea about old ladies attacking young men, but now it's just got SILLY!

Sergeant-Major stops the show after the "Hell's Grannies" sketch, *Monty Python's Flying Circus*, 1969–1974.

NIPPLES EXPLODING WITH DELIGHT

> We find your American beer like making love in a canoe. It's fucking close to water.

First Bruce, to the other Bruces, nailing the piss-poor quality of American beer, *Monty Python Live at the Hollywood Bowl*, 1984.

> I always wanted to be an explorer, but it seemed I was doomed to be nothing more than a very silly person.

Michael Palin, *Palin's Travels* website.

IT'S...

CHAPTER
TWO

SHRUBBERIES & ELDERBERRIES

Python's first movie, 1975's The Holy Grail, is a masterpiece of madness that contains multitudes from the very first clip-clop of coconuts.

Within this mud- and myth-soaked chapter, the film's wit and wisdom goes under the microscope as we go galloping for watery tarts and wooden witches, killer rabbits and maternal hamsters*, unrelenting limbless knights, Ni-sayers, European swallows and, of course, all-things Grail-shaped.

Come, Patsy, let's quest!

*Apologies for the farts in your general direction.

SHRUBBERIES & ELDERBERRIES

40 Specially Trained Ecuadorian Mountain Llamas

6 Venezuelan Red Llamas

142 Mexican Whooping Llamas

14 North Chilean Guanacos (Closely Related to the Llama)

Reg Llama of Brixton

76000 Battery Llamas From "Llama-Fresh" Farms Ltd. Near Paraguay.

and

Terry Gilliam and Terry Jones

The credited directors that roll at the end of *Monty Python and the Holy Grail*. The llamas are still awaiting royalties.

> **O Knights of Ni, you are just and fair, and we will return with a shrubbery.***

King Arthur, on the excessive demands of the Knights of Ni, *Monty Python and the Holy Grail*, 1975.

* One that looks nice, and not too expensive.

SHRUBBERIES & ELDERBERRIES

It was Michael Palin's stroke of genius to use coconuts to imitate the sound of horses on *Holy Grail*. Necessity, however, was the mother of this particular invention. The Pythons could not afford real horses, so they borrowed the idea from the BBC's radio practice of using coconut halves as sound effects for horses.

> Please! This is supposed to be a happy occasion. Let's not bicker and argue about who killed who.

King of Swamp Castle, to his subject after Sir Lancelot's pointy arrival, who got carried away, *Monty Python and the Holy Grail*, 1975.

SHRUBBERIES & ELDERBERRIES

In 2007, the cast of *Spamalot* – and 5,567 extras – clip-clopped into the *Guinness Book of World Records* when the Two Terrys, Jones and Gilliam, set the record for "Largest coconut orchestra of all time" by banging coconuts together during a rendition of "Always Look on the Bright Side of Life". How Pythonesque!

> Oh, wicked, bad, naughty Zoot! She has been setting a light to our beacon, which, I've just remembered, is Grail-shaped. It's not the first time we've had this problem.

Dingo, on her sister Zoot, *Monty Python and the Holy Grail*, 1975.

SHRUBBERIES & ELDERBERRIES

> I warned you, but did you listen to me? Oh, no, you knew, didn't you? Oh, it's just a harmless little bunny, isn't it?

Tim the Enchanter, on the killer rabbit of Caerbannog, *Monty Python and the Holy Grail*, 1975.

> When I first came here, this was all swamp. Everyone said I was daft to build a castle on a swamp, but I built it all the same, just to show them. It sank into the swamp. So I built a second one. That sank into the swamp. So I built a third. That burned down, fell over, then sank into the swamp. But the fourth one stayed up. And that's what you're going to get, lad, the strongest castle in all of England.

King of Swamp Castle, on his son/daughter's Swamp Castle inheritance, *Monty Python and the Holy Grail*, 1975.

SHRUBBERIES & ELDERBERRIES

> You don't frighten us, English pig dogs. Go and boil your bottoms, you sons of a silly person. I blow my nose at you, so-called 'Arthur King', you and all your silly English kaniggats.

French Soldier, insulting King Arthur, *Monty Python and the Holy Grail*, 1975.

> You must cut down the mightiest tree in the forest... WITH... A HERRING!

Knight 1, on the excessive demands of the Knights of Ni, *Monty Python and the Holy Grail*, 1975.

SHRUBBERIES & ELDERBERRIES

Arthur's army at the end of *Holy Grail* is made up of just 175 students from Scotland's University of Stirling.

Each were paid £2 for the day.

> **Are you suggesting that coconuts migrate?**

Guard, on King Arthur's questioning of his employment of coconuts, *Monty Python and the Holy Grail*, 1975.

SHRUBBERIES & ELDERBERRIES

> **Must be a king…
> He hasn't got shit
> all over him.**

Dead Collector, on a passing King Arthur's cleanliness, *Monty Python and the Holy Grail*, 1975.

> I told you, we're an anarcho-syndicalist commune. We take it in turns to act as sort of executive officer for the week but all the decisions of that officer have to be ratified at a special bi-weekly meeting by a simple majority in the case of purely internal affairs but by a two thirds majority…

Dennis, explaining to King Arthur how his peoples are not an autonomous collective, *Monty Python and the Holy Grail*, 1975.

SHRUBBERIES & ELDERBERRIES

> Listen. Strange women lying in ponds distributing swords is no basis for a system of government. Supreme executive power derives from a mandate from the masses, not from some farcical aquatic ceremony. You can't expect to wield supreme executive power just 'cause some watery tart threw a sword at you! I mean, if I went around saying I was an emperor just because some moistened bint had lobbed a scimitar at me, they'd put me away!

Dennis, to King Arthur, about the whole Lady of the Lake legend, *Monty Python and the Holy Grail*, 1975.

" 'Tis but a scratch. "

Black Knight, the stupid bastard, after King Arthur cut him with more than a flesh wound, *Monty Python and the Holy Grail*, 1975.

SHRUBBERIES & ELDERBERRIES

> I don't want to talk to you no more, you empty-headed animal-food trough-wiper! I fart in your general direction! Your mother was a hamster and your father smelt of elderberries!

French Guard, insulting King Arthur at the entrance of the castle, *Monty Python and the Holy Grail*, 1975.

> On second thought,
> let's not go to Camelot.
> It is a silly place.

King Arthur, after a montage of silliness, *Monty Python and the Holy Grail*, 1975.

SHRUBBERIES & ELDERBERRIES

> # An African or a European swallow?

King Arthur, on knowing the difference of air-speed velocity of an unladen African/European swallow, *Monty Python and the Holy Grail*, 1975.

> I am an enchanter. There are some who call me… Tim.

Tim, the enchanter, introduces himself, *Monty Python and the Holy Grail*, 1975.

SHRUBBERIES & ELDERBERRIES

> Oh, what sad times are these when passing ruffians can say 'Ni' at will to old ladies. There is a pestilence upon this land, nothing is sacred. Even those who arrange and design shrubberies are under considerable economic stress at this period in history.

Roger, the shrubber, on King Arthur's Ni-ing to an old peasant woman, *Monty Python and the Holy Grail*, 1975.

* Shrubberies are Roger's trade – he's a shrubber. His name is Roger the Shrubber. He arranges, designs and sells shrubberies.

> I wave my private parts at your aunties, you heaving lot of second-hand electric donkey bottom-biters.

French guard slings one final insult at King Arthur and his kaniggets, *Monty Python and the Holy Grail*, 1975.

SHRUBBERIES & ELDERBERRIES

Elvis Presley was a huge Monty Python fan, particularly *Holy Grail* and the 'Knights Who Say Ni', the forest-dwelling knights who require King Arthur to fetch a shrubbery and cut down a tree with a herring. "We heard Elvis used to take his boys to the local cinema to see it," Eric Idle revealed to *Rolling Stone*.

PYTHONESQUE

Monty Python's influence on comedy and culture became so prevalent that the word to describe their antics and style of humour was added to the English dictionary. Pythonesque is defined as:

"Denoting or resembling the absurdist or surrealist humour or style of Monty Python's Flying Circus, a British television comedy series."

> Ekki-ekki-ekki-ekki-PTANG.
> Zoom-Boing, z'nourrwringmm!

The new phrase of the Knights Who Until Recently Said Ni, told to King Arthur upon his return with a shrubbery, *Monty Python and the Holy Grail*, 1975.

> And the Lord spake, saying, 'First shalt thou take out the Holy Pin. Then shalt thou count to three, no more, no less. Three shall be the number thou shalt count, and the number of the counting shall be three. Four shalt thou not count, neither count thou two, excepting that thou then proceed to three. Five is right out. Once the number three, being the third number, be reached, then lobbest thou thy Holy Hand Grenade of Antioch towards thy foe, who, being naughty in My sight, shall snuff it'.

Cleric, to Brother Maynard, pre-lobbest of thy Holy Hand Grenade of Antioch at the killer rabbit of Caerbannog, *Monty Python and the Holy Grail*, 1975.

SHRUBBERIES & ELDERBERRIES

> If she weighed the same as a duck… she's made of wood.

Peasant 1, to King Arthur and Sir Bedivere, uses logic to solve the witch/duck issue, *Monty Python and the Holy Grail*, 1975.

> You've got two empty halves of coconut and you're bangin' 'em together.

A guard clarifies that coconuts are poor substitutions for horses, *Monty Python and the Holy Grail*, 1975.

SHRUBBERIES & ELDERBERRIES

> I'm French. Why do you think I have this outrageous accent, you silly king?

French guard, to King Arthur, justifying his accent, *Monty Python and the Holy Grail*, 1975.

> I'd given us a rather bad ending for *Holy Grail*, which my daughter still says is the shittiest ending of any film ever.

Eric Idle, on *Holy Grail's* abrupt climax, interview with Donald Liebenson, *Vanity Fair*, August 2, 2019.

SHRUBBERIES & ELDERBERRIES

> **That's enough music for now, lads.**

Brave Sir Robin, after being sung at by his minstrels that he was not in the least bit scared to be mashed into a pulp, or to have his eyes gouged out and his elbows broken, or to have his kneecaps split and his body burned away, and his limbs all hacked and mangled, or his head smashed in and his heart cut out and his liver removed, and his bowels unplugged, and his nostrils raped and his bottom burnt off, and his penis…, *Monty Python and the Holy Grail*, 1975.

> I am afraid our life must seem very dull and quiet compared to yours. We are but eight score young blondes and brunettes, all between sixteen and nineteen and a half, cut off in this castle with no one to protect us! Oh, it is a lonely life – bathing, dressing, undressing, making exciting underwear… We are just not used to handsome knights.

Zoot goes looking for a spanking after Galahad's desire for a little bit of "peril", *Monty Python and the Holy Grail*, 1975.

SHRUBBERIES & ELDERBERRIES

> Oh, anyway, on to scene twenty-four, which is a smashing scene with some lovely acting, in which Arthur discovers a vital clue, in which there aren't any swallows, although I think you can hear a starling.

The narrator narrating terribly, *Monty Python and the Holy Grail*, 1975.

Monty Python and the Holy Grail was part-financed by several of the world's greatest rock bands, including Led Zeppelin (who contributed £31,500, or £336,000 today), Pink Floyd (£21,000/£224,000), and Jethro Tull frontman Ian Anderson, who put in £6,300/£67,000 of his own money. The film was considered a good tax write-off as rock stars paid 90 per cent income tax.

SHRUBBERIES & ELDERBERRIES

> We dine well here in Camelot. We eat ham and jam and spam a lot.

Knights of Camelot, in full song, discussing Camelot and giving rise to a future award-winning Broadway phenomenon, *Monty Python and the Holy Grail*, 1975.

> # Alright, sonny, that's enough. Pack it in.

Policeman, as he stops the Two Terrys filming, ending the medieval movie abruptly in the modern day, *Monty Python and the Holy Grail*, 1975.

INTERMISSION

Hello, and welcome to "The Middle of the Book". We're going to take moment now to take a break to invite you, the reader, to join us, the publishers, in "Find the Fish".

Somewhere in this book there is a fish. Can you find it?*

*You get nothing for finding it by the way. There's no prize.***

** If we're honest, the only reason we're doing this is we're just desperately squirming for things to include and this idea seemed better than just having a blank double page for you to doodle on, which is what the Publisher suggested but everybody in Sales and Marketing thought was a terrible idea.*

IT'S...

CHAPTER THREE

MOVE OVER JEHOVAH

❦

Onwards we venture into Pythonland! This time to Jerusalem, 2,000 years ago, give or take an AD or two.

It was a time of cheesemakers and crucifixions, aliens and blasphemers, prophets and disciples, and, of course, naughty boys called Brian whose lust for glory is now legendary.

Monty Python's magnum opus, 1979's *Life of Brian*, is regularly ranked as one of the Greatest Comedy Films of All Time™, and rightly so, as the creators of its funniest lines will now reveal. Let's *eunt**...

**The third person plural present indicative of "go", remember.*

MOVE OVER JEHOVAH

> Alright, but apart from the sanitation, the medicine, education, wine, public order, irrigation, roads, the fresh-water system, and public health, what have the Romans ever done for us?

Reg, on the dreadful effectiveness of the Romans, The People's Front of Judea*, *Life of Brian*, 1979.

Not the Judean People's Front!

> When we made *Life of Brian*, which I think is definitely our best work, it just happened that we all pretty much agreed on what religion wasn't. If we'd tried to agree on what religion should be, we would have always been arguing and unable to reach a common viewpoint. When you're dealing with humour, it's very simple: Is it funny or not?

John Cleese, on *Life of Brian*, *Harvard Business Review*, March 2014.

MOVE OVER JEHOVAH

> What Jesus blatantly fails to appreciate is that it's the meek who are the problem.

Reg, to Francis and Judith, about Jesus's Sermon on the Mount, *Life of Brian*, 1979.

> Look, you've got it all wrong! You don't need to follow me. You don't need to follow anybody! You've got to think for yourselves! You're all individuals!

Brian's wise words fall on deaf ears, *Life of Brian*, 1979.

MOVE OVER JEHOVAH

12

The number, in both *Holy Grail* and *Life of Brian*, of characters played by Michael Palin, the highest by a Python.

Can you guess them all?

JESUS CHRIST: LUST FOR GLORY

Life of Brian's original title, developed from an off-the-cuff comment by Eric Idle at the premiere of *Monty Python and the Holy Grail* in New York, when asked by a journalist about the team's next movie.

MOVE OVER JEHOVAH

> He's not the Messiah.
> He's a very naughty boy!
> Now, go away!

Virgin Mandy, Brian's mother, offers the film's most iconic line, *Life of Brian*, 1979.

> Once I was moaning a little bit on the set of *Brian*, telling George Harrison, 'It was hard to get onscreen with Michael Palin and John Cleese.' He said, 'Well, imagine what it's like trying to get studio time with Lennon and McCartney.' I said, 'All right. Absolutely. Got it. OK. Check. I'll shut up now.' Then it occurred to me that, yes, in fact, we were slightly the outsiders, playing similar roles in our groups.

Eric Idle, on being the George Harrison of the Beatles of Comedy, interview with Kory Grow, *Rolling Stone*, 2018.

MOVE OVER JEHOVAH

> And the beast shall be huge and black, and the eyes thereof red with the blood of living creatures, and the whore of Babylon shall ride forth on a three-headed serpent, and throughout the lands, there'll be a great rubbing of parts.

Blood and Thunder Prophet tells the crowd what they want to hear, *Life of Brian*, 1979.

After many religious groups in the U.S. protested against *Life of Brian*, the number of screens showing the film tripled from 200 to 600 due to media exposure, ensuring more people went to see it. "They actually made me rich," John Cleese said of the protesters, to the BBC. "I feel we should send them a crate of champagne or something."

MOVE OVER JEHOVAH

> # Blessed are the cheesemakers.

A man mishears Jesus's Sermon on the Mount, a sentence not to be taken literally, it refers to any dairy product manufacturers, *Life of Brian*, 1979.

> I'd had a lovely supper, and all I said to my wife was, 'That piece of halibut was good enough for Jehovah.'

The blasphemous Mattias, son of Deuteronomy of Gath, before his scheduled stoning by the definitely not-female over-zealous stoners, *Life of Brian*, 1979.

MOVE OVER JEHOVAH

> Four hundred years ago, we would have been burnt for this film. Now, I'm suggesting that we've made an advance.

John Cleese, defending *Life of Brian* on BBC's *Friday Night, Saturday Morning* to Christian apologist Malcolm Muggeridge, November 9, 1979.

> I'm not oppressing you, Stan. You haven't got a womb! Where's the foetus gonna gestate? You gonna keep it in a box?

Reg discusses the issues of trans rights with Stan (Loretta), *Life of Brian*, 1979.

MOVE OVER JEHOVAH

Romani Ite Domum.*
(Romans Go Home)

What Brian should have graffitied instead of *Romanes eunt domus*.

(People called Romanes, they go the house)*

> **Anybody else feel like a little giggle when I mention my fwiend… Biggus…Dickus?***

Pontius Pilate defends his friend Biggus Dickus, *Life of Brian*, 1979.

* Incontinentia Buttocks is the name of Biggus Dickus's wife, FYI.

MOVE OVER JEHOVAH

> **All right, I am the Messiah! Now, fuck off!***

Brian grows aggravated by the paradoxical nature of his disciples, *Life of Brian*, 1979.

* To which a disciple responds hilariously, "How shall we fuck off, oh Lord?"

> We thought quite hard and carefully about *Life of Brian*, because of the subject matter, because it was about religion. We were all grown-up enough to know that you could get into difficult areas if it was just seen to be jokes about the Bible and Christ falling off donkeys.

Michael Palin, on *Life of Brian*, interviewed by Alex Musson, *Mustard*, 2005.

MOVE OVER JEHOVAH

> **We can see you're not Jewish.**

When it came to Brian's nude scene in *Life of Brian*, it became immediately evident that Graham Chapman was not circumcised. To solve the issue, Graham tied a rubber band around his foreskin. Go see for yourself.

> What are you doing creeping around a cow shed at two o'clock in the morning? That doesn't sound very wise to me.

The Virgin Mandy makes a point with the Three Wise Men, *Life of Brian*, 1979.

MOVE OVER JEHOVAH

> I was hopping along, minding my own business, all of a sudden, up Jesus comes, cures me! One minute I'm a leper with a trade, next minute my livelihood's gone. Not so much as a by-your-leave! 'You're cured, mate.' Bloody do-gooder.

The Ex-Leper complains about Jesus's miraculous healing powers, *Life of Brian*, 1979.

> I was only bothered by the criticism [of *Life of Brian*] because of everybody thinking that whatever God they believe in doesn't have a sense of humour.

Graham Chapman, on criticism for *Life of Brian*, *New York Times*, 1976.

MOVE OVER JEHOVAH

> It's the end of the film. Incidentally, this record's available in the foyer. Some of us have got to live as well, you know. Who do you think pays for all this rubbish?

Mr Frisbee III invites the audience to buy the single "Always Look on the Bright Side of Life" as they exit the cinema, *Life of Brian*, 1979.

> Let me come with you, Pontiuth. I may be of thome athithtanthe if there ith a thudden crithith!

Biggus Dickus's speech impediment doesn't stop him telling Pontius Pilate that he may be of some assistance if there is a sudden crisis, *Life of Brian*, 1979.

MOVE OVER JEHOVAH

> **Oh, it's blessed are the meek! Oh, I'm glad they're getting something, they have a hell of a time.**

Mrs Big Nose finally understands what Jesus is banging on about up the mount, *Life of Brian*, 1979.

> What I was thinking was, I was going to ask him if he could make me a bit lame in one leg during the middle of the week. You know, something beggable, but not leprosy, which is a pain in the ass to be blunt.

The Ex-Leper tells Brain of his plan to ask Jesus to perform another miracle, *Life of Brian*, 1979.

$4 MILLION

The amount Beatles guitarist George Harrison gave to the Pythons to complete the filming of *Life of Brian*. Terry Jones described it as "the most expensive movie ticket of all time" after Harrison said he simply wanted to watch the movie after reading the script. Harrison remortgaged his house in order to ensure the film was made, after its original financier pulled out. *Life of Brian* was a huge hit, earning $20 million at the box office.

> # He wanks as high as any in Wome!

Pontius Pilate gives his friend Biggus Dickus a shout-out to the sniggering crowd, *Life of Brian*, 1979.

MOVE OVER JEHOVAH

> I thought at least getting the Catholics, Protestants and Jews all protesting against our movie was fairly ecumenical on our part. We had achieved something useful.

Terry Gilliam

> We don't deliberately set out to offend. Unless we feel it's justified. And in the case of certain well-known religions, it was justified.

Graham Chapman, on offence, *New York Times*, 1976.

MOVE OVER JEHOVAH

> All our characters were heading for crucifixion; how do you find an end to that in a comedy? So my suggestion was we'll finish with a song. I had an instinct it should be like a Disney whistle song. We should be cheery and upbeat… It went into the script that day as 'I'm Looking on the Bright Side', and then I went home and wrote it immediately in about an hour.

Eric Idle, on "Always Look on the Bright Side of Life", interview with Donald Liebenson, *Vanity Fair*, August 2, 2019.

> **I'm Brian, and so's my wife!**

Gregory gets behind Brian, *Life of Brian*, 1979.

MOVE OVER JEHOVAH

> There's no Messiah in here. There's a mess all right, but no Messiah.

Virgin Mandy to the swarming crowd outside her house, *Life of Brian*, 1979.

> Oh, not like these, sir. Look at this. Feel the quality of that. That's craftsmanship, sir.

Harry the Haggler tries to convince Virgin Mandy to buy his premium stones, *Life of Brian*, 1979.

MOVE OVER JEHOVAH

During the filming of the "Biggus Dickus" sketch in *Life of Brian*, Michael Palin used a different punchline every time to ensure the laughter of the Roman guard extras in the background was genuine. The guards were told that if they laughed during a take they would not get paid.

> We always stated *Life of Brian* wasn't blasphemous, but heretical. It wasn't about what Christ was saying, but about the people who followed Him – the ones who for the next 2,000 years would torture and kill each other because they couldn't agree on what He was saying about peace and love.

Terry Jones, on *Life of Brian*, interview with Nathan Bevan, Wales Online, March 5, 2011.

MOVE OVER JEHOVAH

> From now on you shall be called Brian that is called Brian.

Reg welcomes Brian into the People's Front of Judea*, *Life of Brian*, 1979.

*Not the Judean People's Front!

In a 2014 study by a chain of funeral directors, it was revealed that the most popular tune to play at a UK funeral was "Always Look on the Bright Side of Life", followed (somewhat ironically) by "The Lord is My Shepherd".

MOVE OVER JEHOVAH

Larks' tongues
Wrens' livers
Chaffinch brains
Jaguars' earlobes
Wolf nipple chips
Dromedary pretzels
Tuscany fried bats
Otters' noses
Ocelot spleens

"Get 'em while they're hot.
They're lovely."

The "Roman rubbish" Brian sells at the Colosseum, Jerusalem.

While promoting *Life of Brian*, the gang used funny taglines to sell the film on movie posters:

1. A motion picture destined to offend nearly two thirds of the civilized world. And severely annoy the other third!

2. See the movie that's controversial, sacrilegious, and blasphemous. But if that's not playing, see *Life of Brian*.

3. Honk if you love Brian.

4. The film that is so funny it was banned in Norway.

5. Just when you thought you were saved…

6. Makes *Ben-Hur* look like an epic.

MOVE OVER JEHOVAH

> **Welease Woger!**

Bob Hoskins (the character's name!) widicules Pontius Pilate, *Life of Brian*, 1979.

> I'm only joking. I'm not really Brian. No, I'm not Brian. I'm only pulling your leg! It's a joke! I'm not him! I'm just having you on! Put me back! Bloody Romans! Can't take a joke!

Mr Cheeky commits an act of identity theft on the cross, *Life of Brian*, 1979.

IT'S...

CHAPTER FOUR

SPERMALOT

Monty Python's The Meaning of Life (1983) is as messy, hilarious, absurd and ludicrous as life itself, and thus is the perfect representation of it.

Stuffed with as many tasty treats as Mr Creosote's mouth, this stream of silliness meanders aimlessly from birth, middle age and death, acting as the last lunacy-filed gasp of Python before the troupe themselves expired, ex-parrot-esque.

Thankfully, the 40-year-old film remains essential viewing, as these iconic catchphrases, quotes and jokes will attest. Ping!

SPERMALOT

> It's not a virus, I'm afraid. You see, a virus is what we doctors call very, very small. So small, it could not possibly have made off with a whole leg. What we're looking for here is, I think, is some multi-cellular life form with stripes, huge razor-sharp teeth, about eleven foot long, and of the genus Felis Horribilis: what we doctors, in fact, call a 'tiger'.

Doctor Livingstone tells Perkins his injury is a little more than but a scratch, *The Meaning of Life*, 1983.

> **Well, of course, warfare isn't all fun!**

Army General, before being struck by the Hand of God, *The Meaning of Life*, 1983.

"

They haven't said much about the meaning of life so far, have they?

"

Fish #2 reviews the film halfway through,
The Meaning of Life, 1983.

* Fish #5 very much doubts if they're going to say anything about the meaning of life at all.

JULY 22, 2014

Monty Python performed the final reunion show, entitled *The Last Night of the Pythons*. It was watched live by a 15,000-strong audience at The O2, London, and simulcast on television to an estimated worldwide audience of 50 million.

> # It's only wafer-thin.

Maître d', to Mr Creosote, seconds before explosion, *The Meaning of Life*, 1983.

> **I see you have the machine that goes 'ping'. This is my favourite.**

Mr Pyecroft delights in the ping machine (the one that means your baby is alive, and cost three quarters of a million pounds), *The Meaning of Life*, 1983.

SPERMALOT

> **You're a Catholic the moment Dad came.**

Dad, before bursting into "Every Sperm is Sacred"*,
The Meaning of Life, 1983.

*Remember: Every sperm is sacred. Every sperm is great.
If a sperm is wasted, God gets quite irate.

> Let us praise God. O Lord, ooh, You are so big, so absolutely huge. Gosh, we're all really impressed down here, I can tell You. Forgive us, O Lord, for this, our dreadful toadying, but You are so strong and, well, just so super.

The Chaplain goes overboard praising the Lord with the barefaced flattery, *The Meaning of Life*, 1983.

SPERMALOT

> **Now, did I or did I not… do… vaginal… juices?***

Humphrey educates his pupils,
The Meaning of Life, 1983.

* *Tonguing will give you the best idea of how the juices are coming along.*

> And, finally, here are some completely gratuitous pictures of penises to annoy the censors and to hopefully spark some sort of controversy, which, it seems, is the only way these days to get the jaded, video-sated public off their fucking arses and back in the sodding cinema. Family entertainment? Bollocks.

The Lady Presenter on family entertainment, *The Meaning of Life*, 1983.

SPERMALOT

1. People doing things to each other with chainsaws during Tupperware parties

2. Babysitters being stabbed with knitting needles by gay presidential candidates

3. Vigilante groups strangling chickens

4. Armed bands of theatre critics exterminating mutant goats

What will get the "jaded, video-sated public off their fucking arses and back in the sodding cinema", *The Meaning of Life*, 1983.

> # Isn't it awfully nice to have a penis?

Nöel Coward (not the real one) beginning "The Penis Song", *The Meaning of Life*, 1983.

> All I know is that, for reasons that none of us understand, Monty Python just seems to go on and on and on. In America, in particular, every new young generation seems to rediscover it, which is a mystery to us.

John Cleese, on the enduring popularity of Python, *Harvard Business Review*, March 2014.

> Englishmen, you're all so fucking pompous. None of you have got any balls.

The Grim Reaper, on Englishmen, *Monty Python's the Meaning of Life*, 1983.

> **Better get a bucket. I'm gonna throw up.**

Mr Creosote informs the Maître d' he is feeling better in a way, *The Meaning of Life*, 1983.

> Protestantism doesn't stop at the simple condom. Oh, no. I can wear French Ticklers* if I want.

Harry Blackitt teases his wife with his religious freedoms, *The Meaning of Life*, 1983.

*Black Mambos and Crocodile Ribs ("Sheaths that are designed not only to protect, but also to enhance the stimulation of sexual congress") too.

SPERMALOT

> The Catholic Church has done some wonderful things in their time. They preserved the might and majesty, even the mystery, of the Church of Rome, the sanctity of the sacrament, and the indivisible oneness of the Trinity. But if they'd let me wear one of those little rubber things on the end of my cock, we wouldn't be in the mess we are now.

Dad, on his family's financial predicament, as he begins to sell his many children off for scientific experiments because of his devoted Catholicism, *The Meaning of Life*, 1983.

> Don't stand there gawpin' like you've never seen the hand of God before!

The kindly Sergeant Major (before dismissing his squadron from walking up and down the square), *The Meaning of Life*, 1983.

SPERMALOT

> We would only do a reunion if Chapman came back from the dead. So we're negotiating with his agent.

Eric Idle, on speculation of a Monty Python reunion, 1996.

43 SECONDS

The time it took for the Monty Python reunion tickets, at their historic London 02 tour in July 2014, to sell out. The tagline for the shows was "One Down, Five To Go".

To promote the reunion, the Python's asked Mick Jagger to say a few nice words: *"Who wants to see that again, really? It's a bunch of wrinkly old men trying to relive their youth and make a load of money – the best one died years ago!"*

SPERMALOT

> If I had not gone into Monty Python, I probably would have stuck to my original plan to graduate and become a chartered accountant, perhaps a barrister lawyer, and gotten a nice house in the suburbs, with a nice wife and kids, and gotten a country club membership, and then I would have killed myself.

John Cleese, on comedy as a career, *Fresh Air*, interview with Terry Gross, 1997.

> Well, that's the end of the film. Now, here's the meaning of life. Well, it's nothing very special. Try and be nice to people, avoid eating fat, read a good book every now and then, get some walking in, and try and live together in peace and harmony with people of all creeds and nations.

The Lady Presenter on the meaning of life, *The Meaning of Life*, 1983.

> For Mr Creosote, I just sat down and wrote a sketch in the worst possible taste. In fact, at the top of the paper it read: "Sketch in the Worst Possible Taste." The first time I ever read that in front of the rest of Python, we had just eaten lunch. No one liked it. But then a month later John Cleese rang me up and said, 'I'm going to change my mind about this.'

Terry Jones, on the "Mr Creosote" sketch, interview with Mike Sacks, *Vulture*, January 2014.

MR CREOSOTE'S MEAL

Appetisers

Moules Mariniere

Pâté de Foie Gras

Beluga Caviar

Eggs Benedictine

Tart De Poireaux ("That's Leek Tart")

Frogs' Legs Amandine

Oeufs De Caille Richard Shepherd

All mixed in a bucket with the quail eggs on top and a double helping of pâté.

Main Course

Jugged Hare with truffles, anchovies, grand marnier, bacon and cream.

Drinks

Six bottles of Château Latour 1945

A double jeroboam of champagne

Half a dozen crates of brown ale

Mr Creosote's entire eating à la carte, plus one wafer-thin mint, *The Meaning of Life*, 1983.

PYTHON PLAYLIST: THE VERY BEST SONGS

"Always Look on the Bright Side of Life"

"Penis Song"

"Finland"

"I'm So Worried"

"Every Sperm is Sacred"

"I Like Chinese"

"Sit On My Face"

"Never Be Rude to an Arab"

"Brian Song"

"Knights of the Round Table"

"All Things Dull and Ugly"

"Decomposing Composers"

"I've Got Two Legs"

"Galaxy Song"

"Spam Song"

"Lumberjack Song"

> I've had a team working on this over the past few weeks, and what we've come up with can be reduced to two fundamental concepts. One, people are not wearing enough hats. Two, matter is energy.

Harry, a suited executive, informs other executives in a corporate boardroom of the meaning of life, *The Meaning of Life*, 1983.

SPERMALOT

1,575

Eric Idle's reimagining of *Holy Grail*, *Spamalot*, was a Broadway phenomenon, running for 1,575 performances from 2005 to 2009. It made almost as much as John Cleese's third wife in their infamous divorce, which led to the Pythons' reunion in 2014.

> It's a 'Mr. Death' or something. He's come about the reaping? I don't think we need any at the moment.

Geoffrey lets the Grim Reaper in to do some reaping, *The Meaning of Life*, 1983.

SPERMALOT

FIN

Stop that, it's silly.